Come In t...

A-1

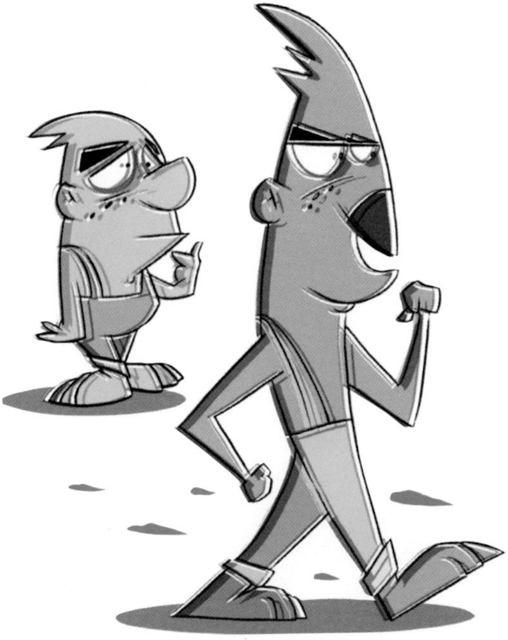

Illustrated by Josh Dobson

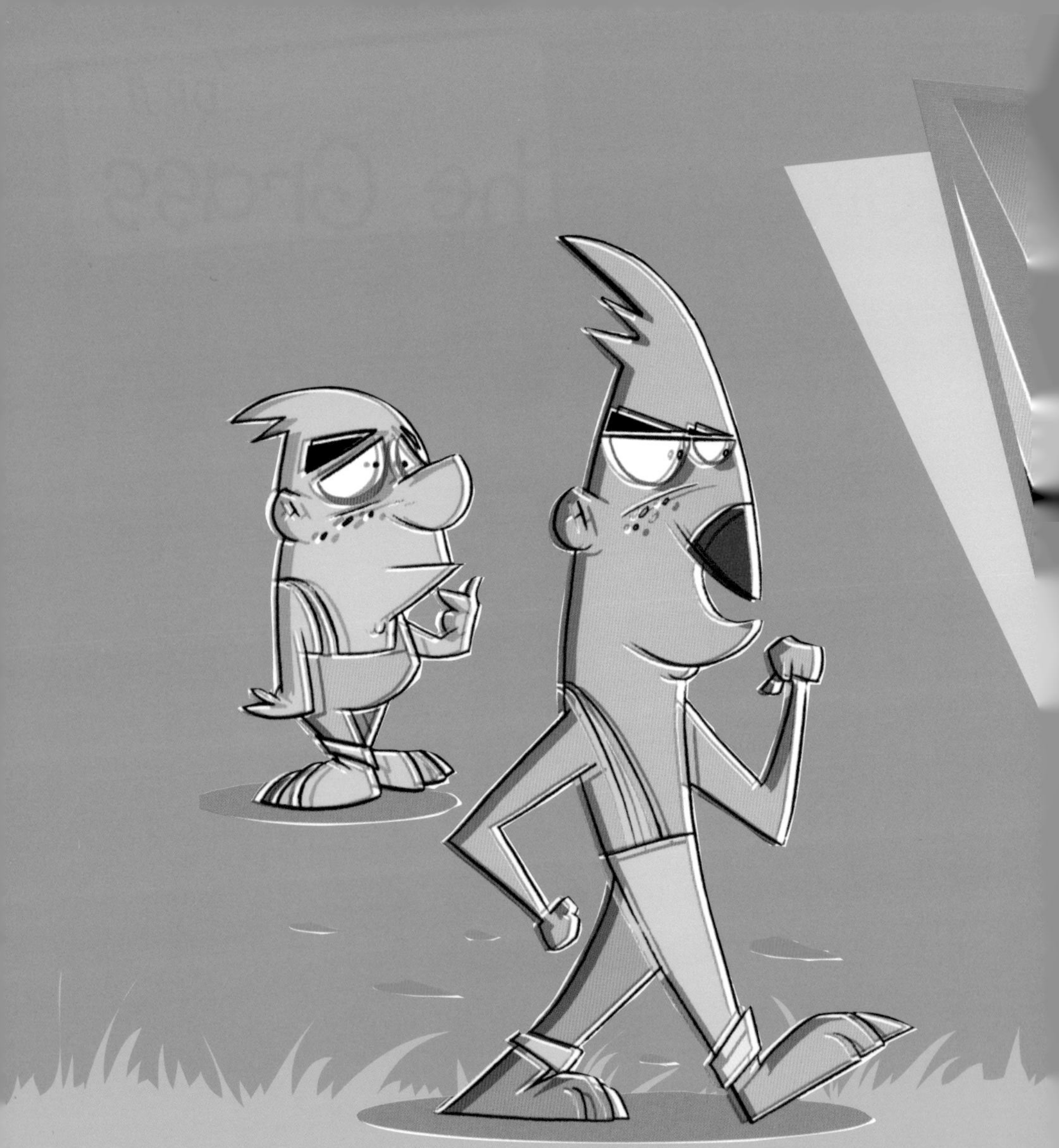

Come in the grass.

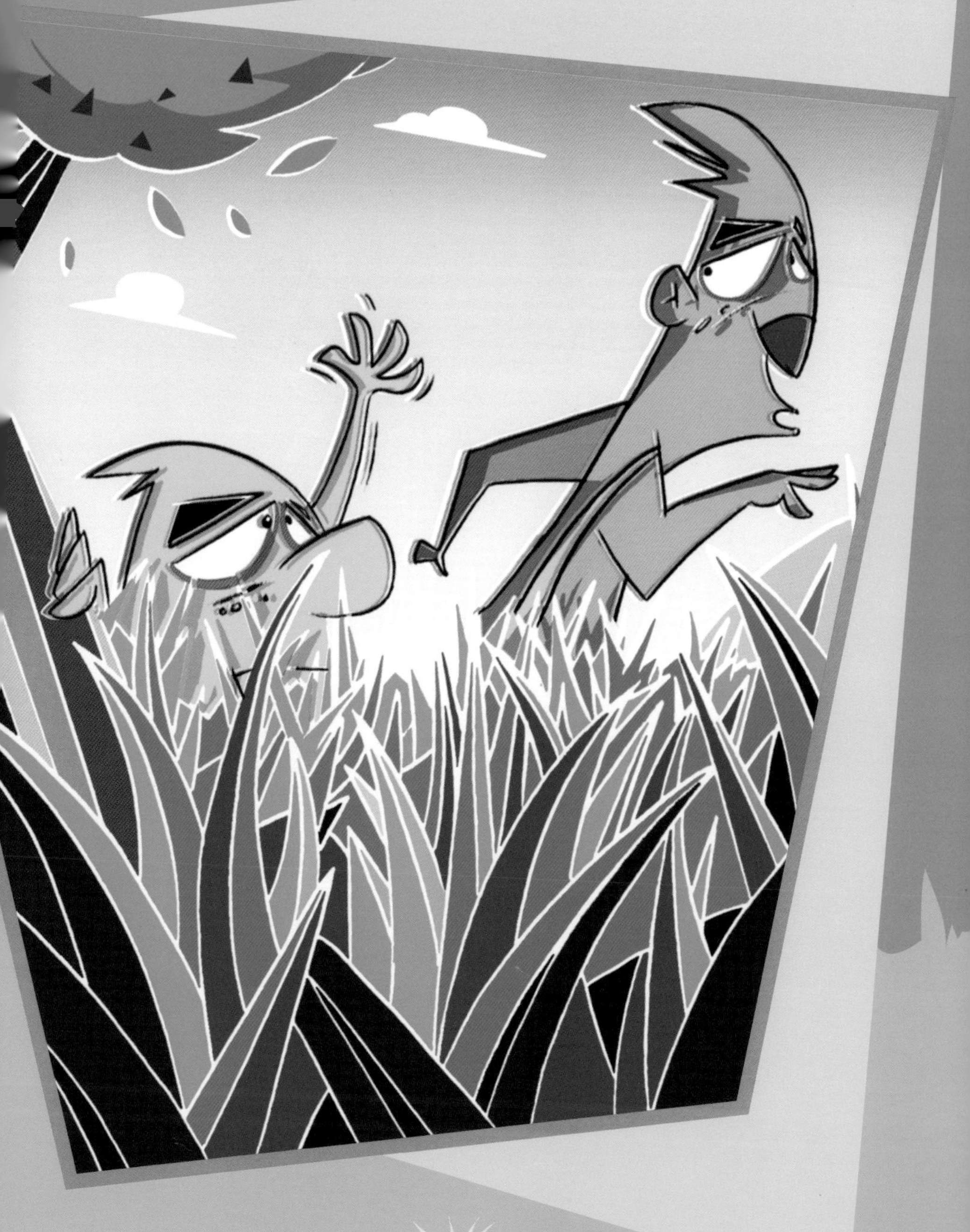

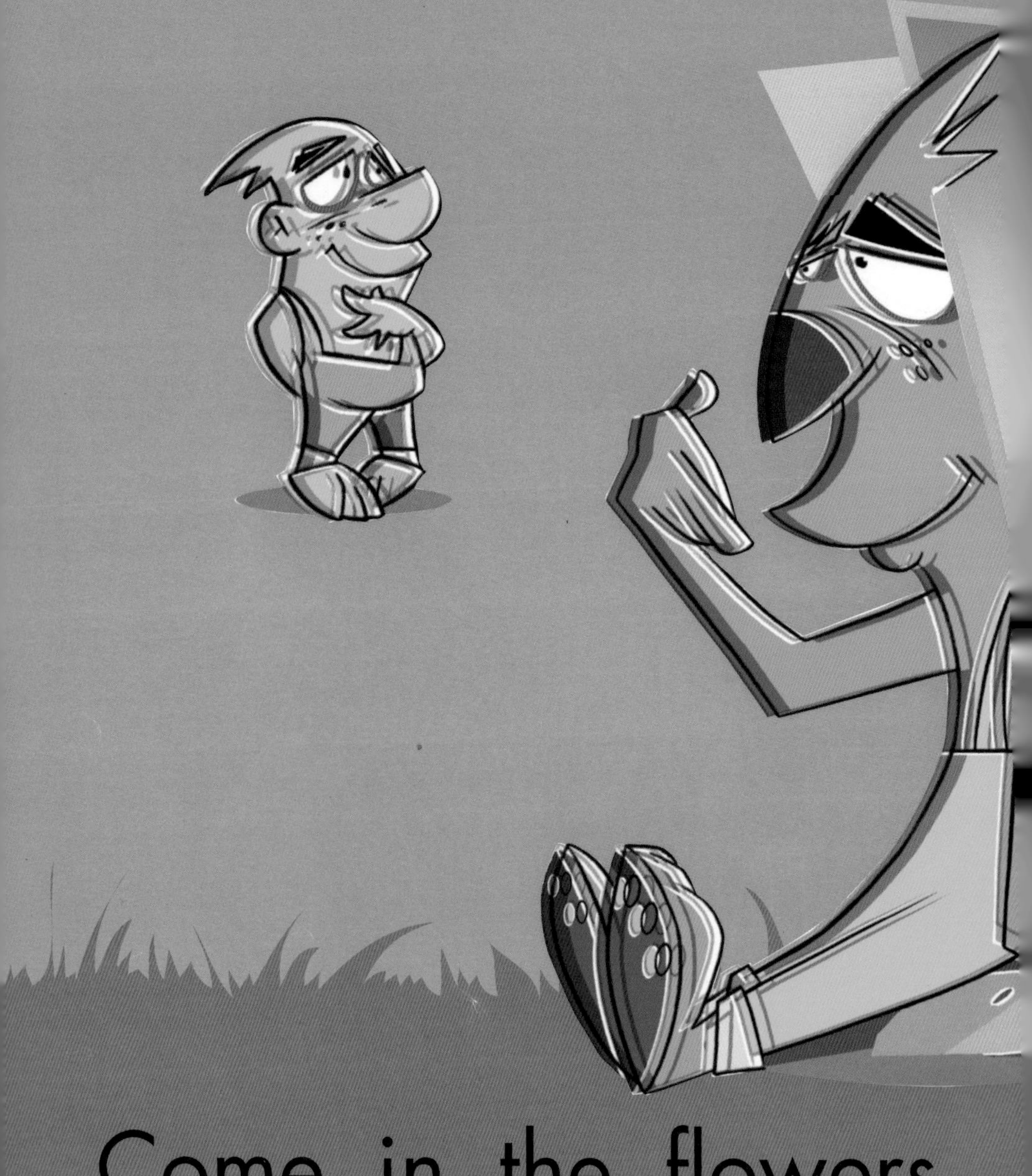

Come in the flowers.

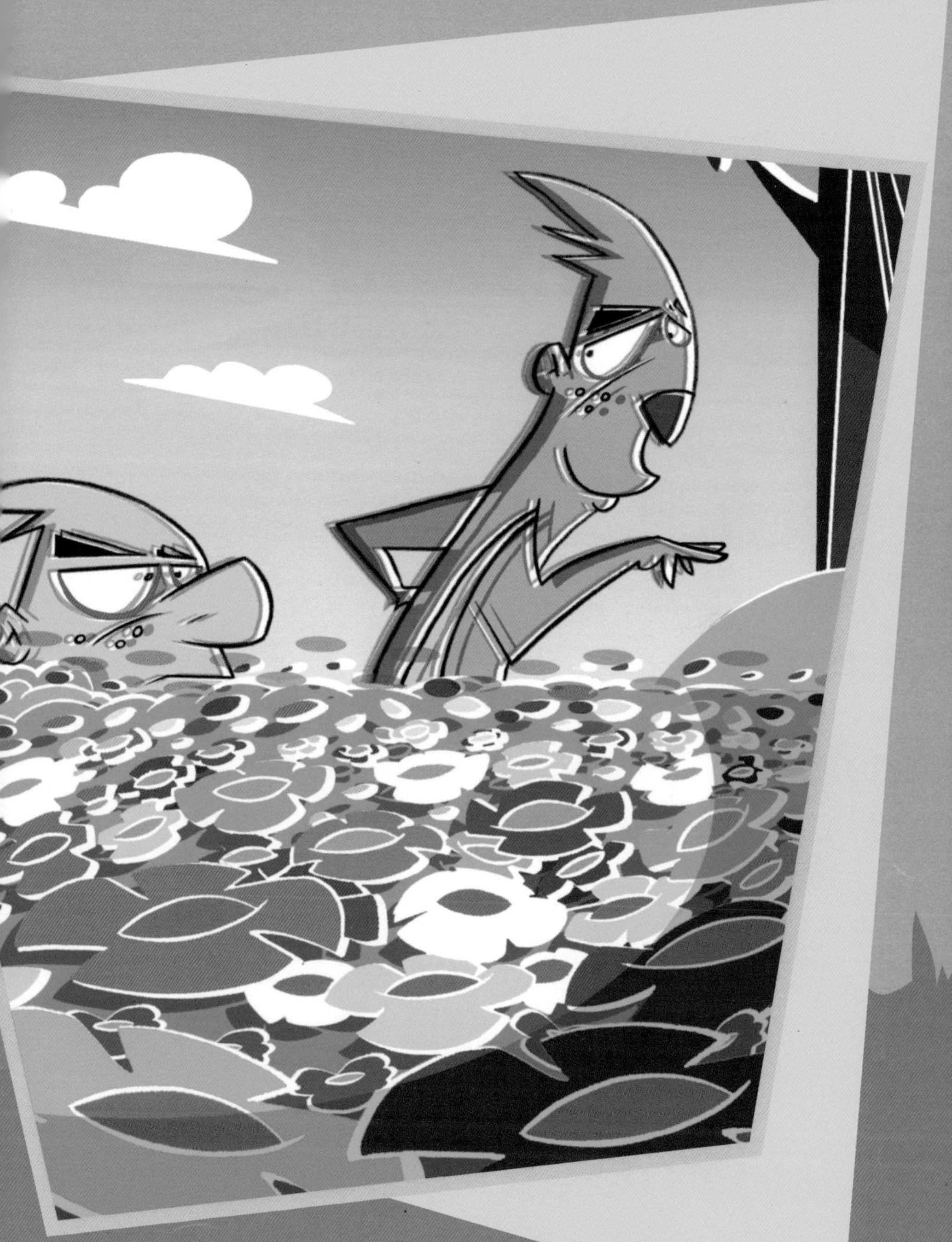

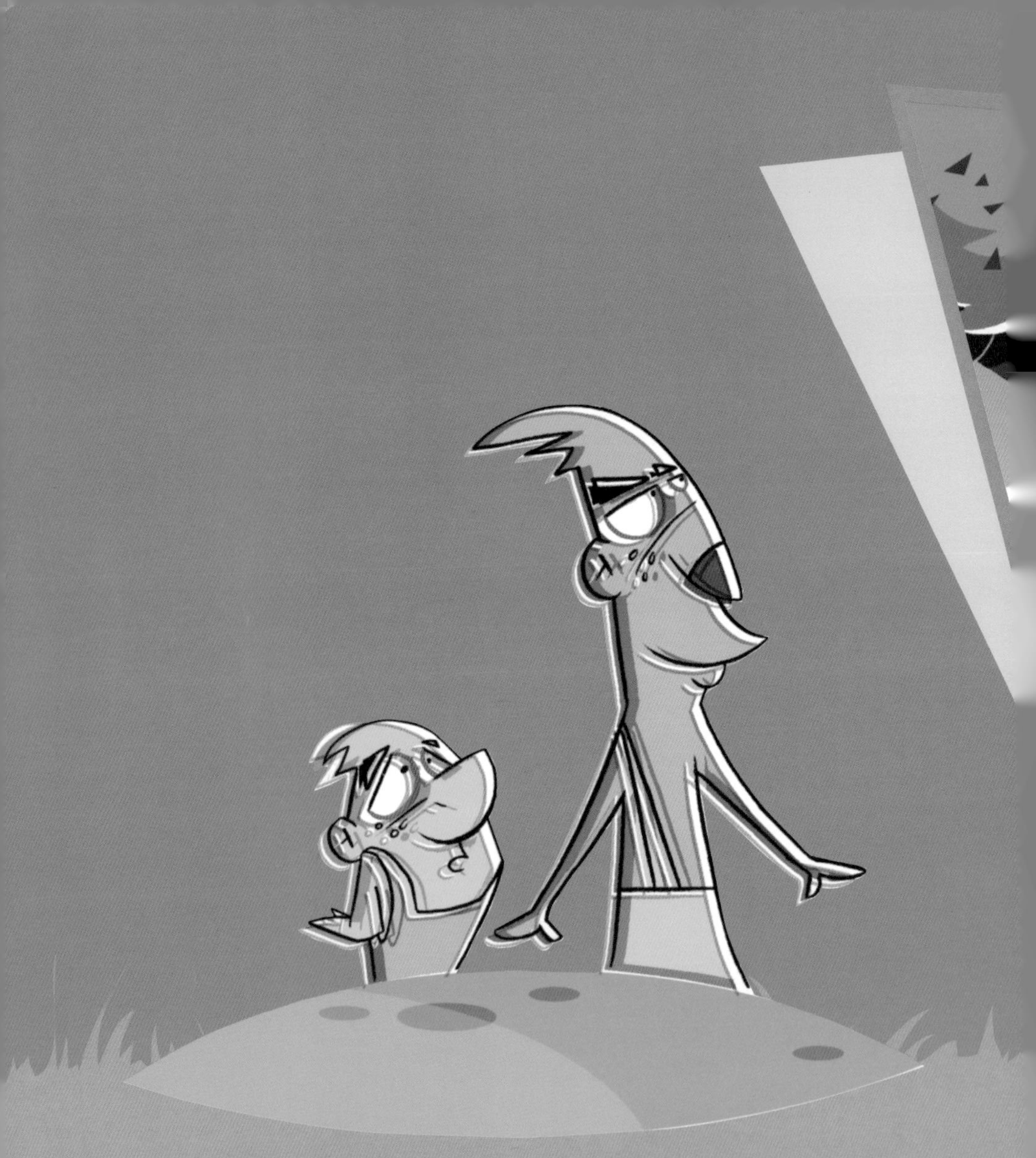

Come in the tree.

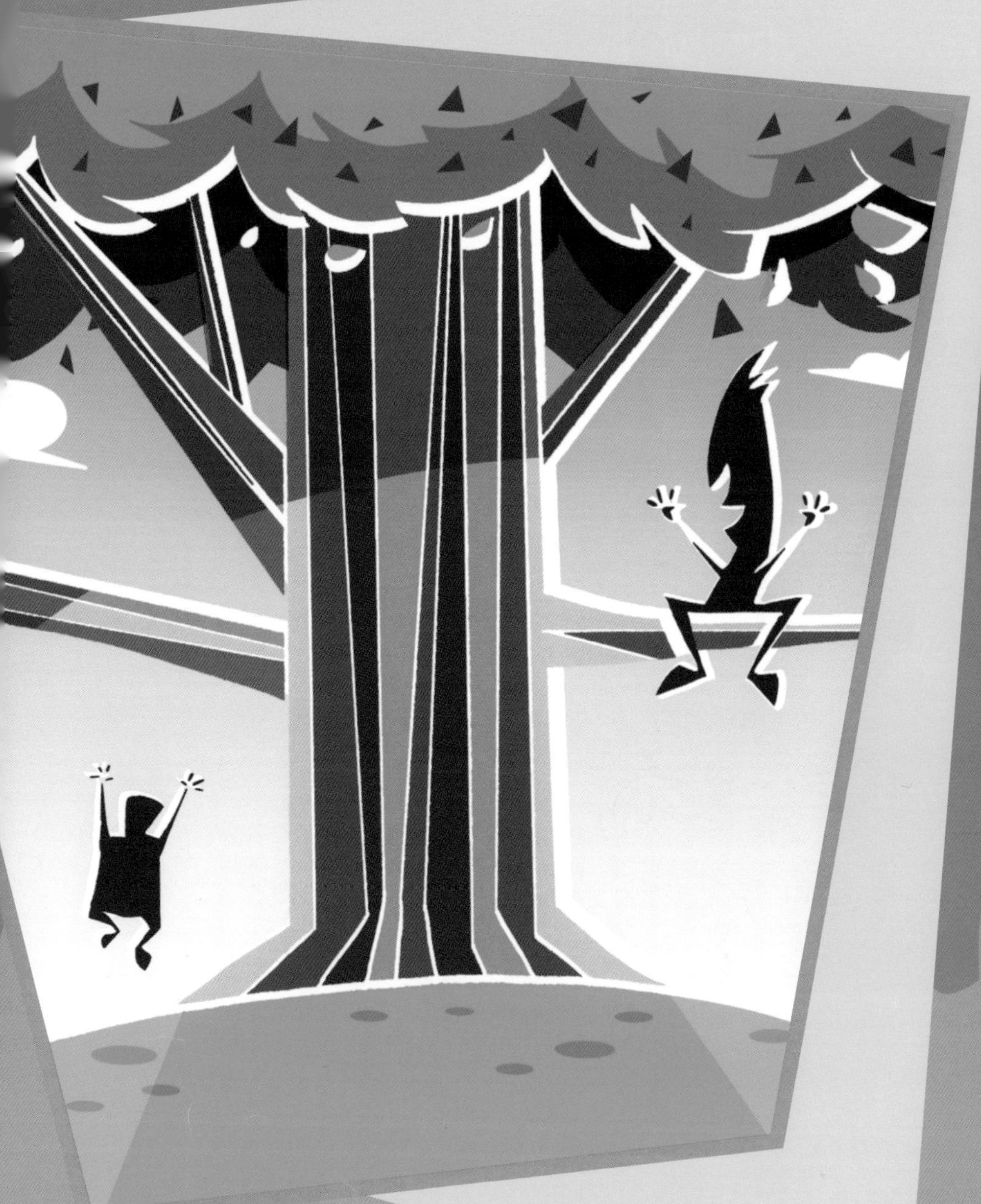

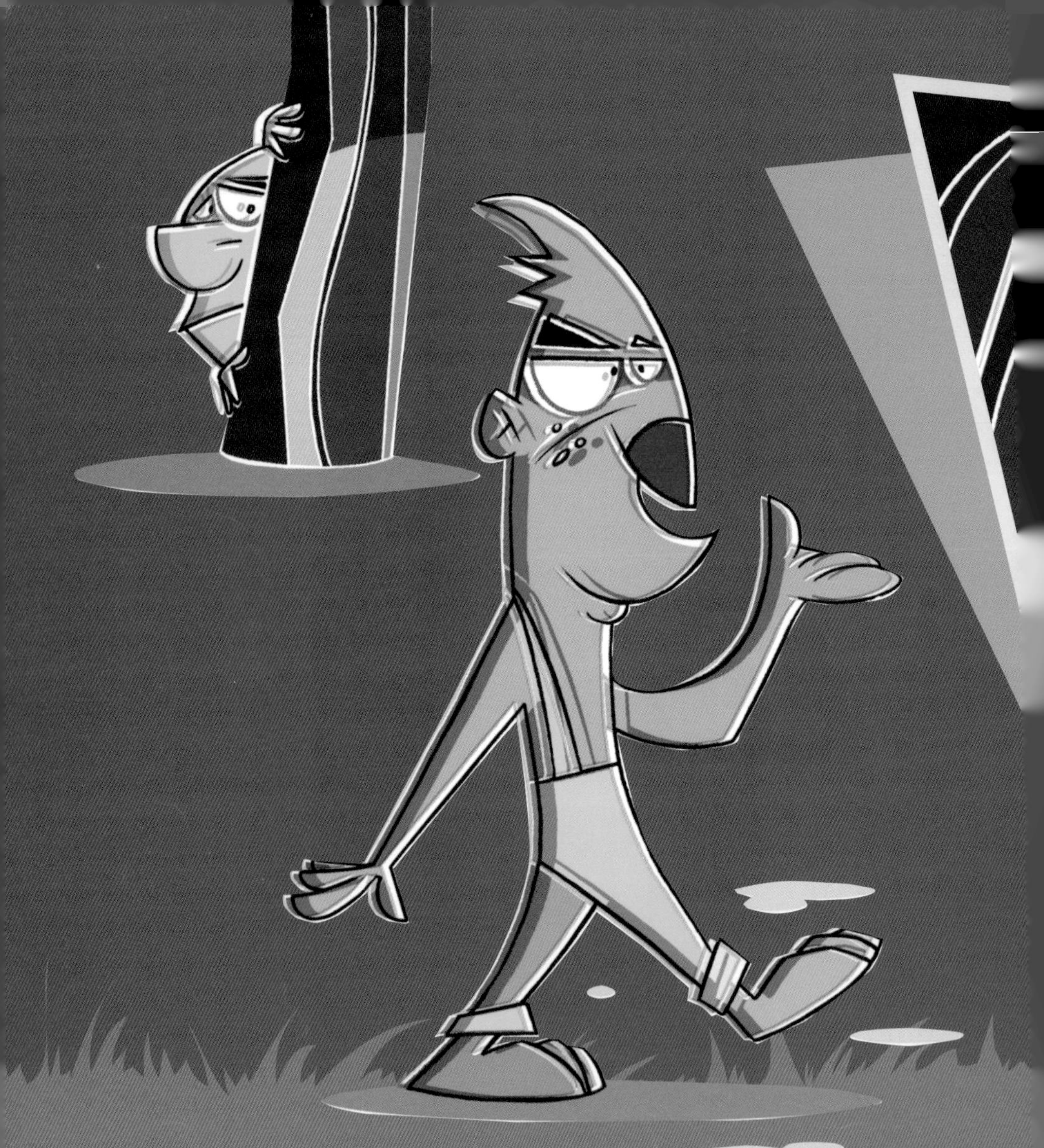

Come in the water.

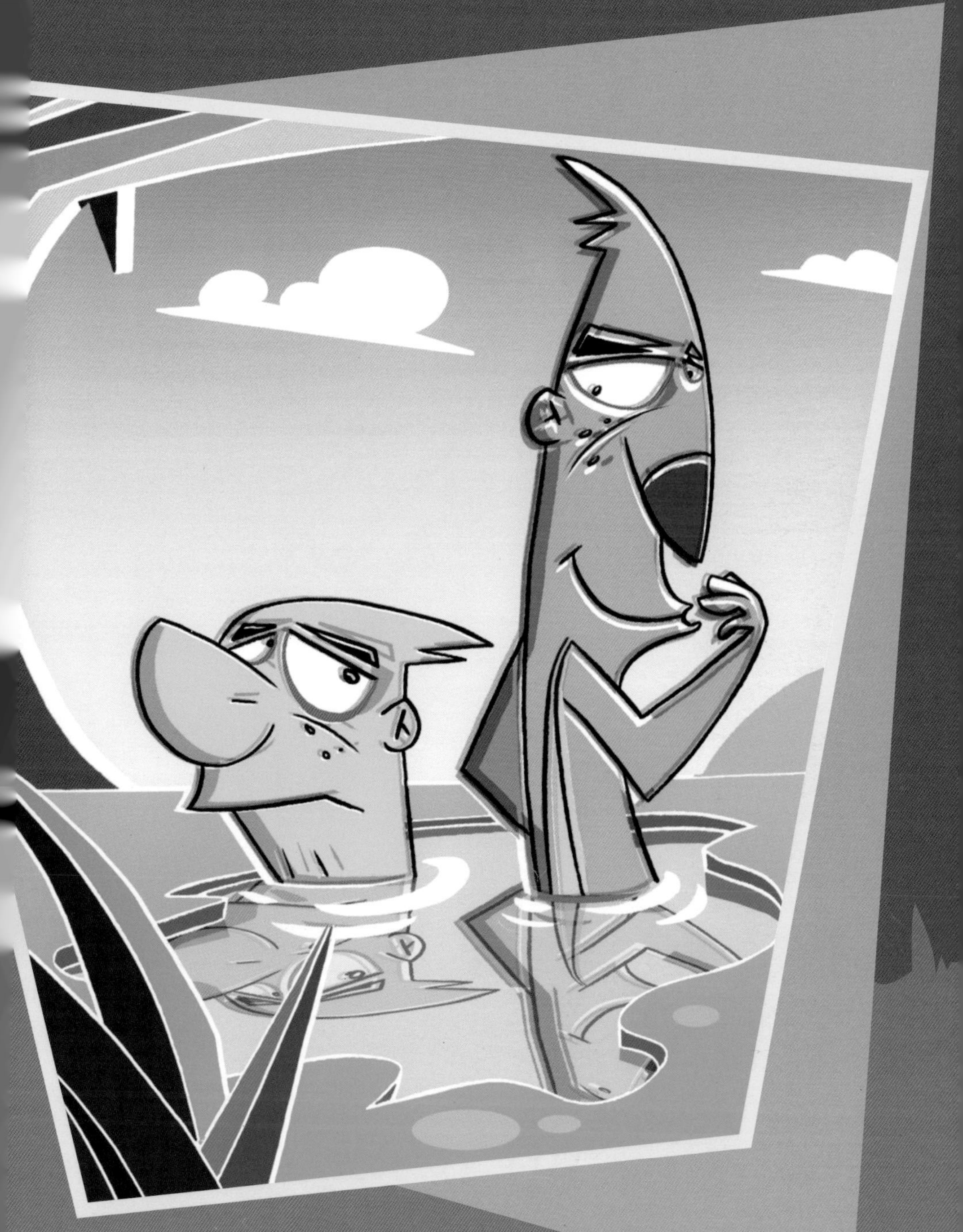

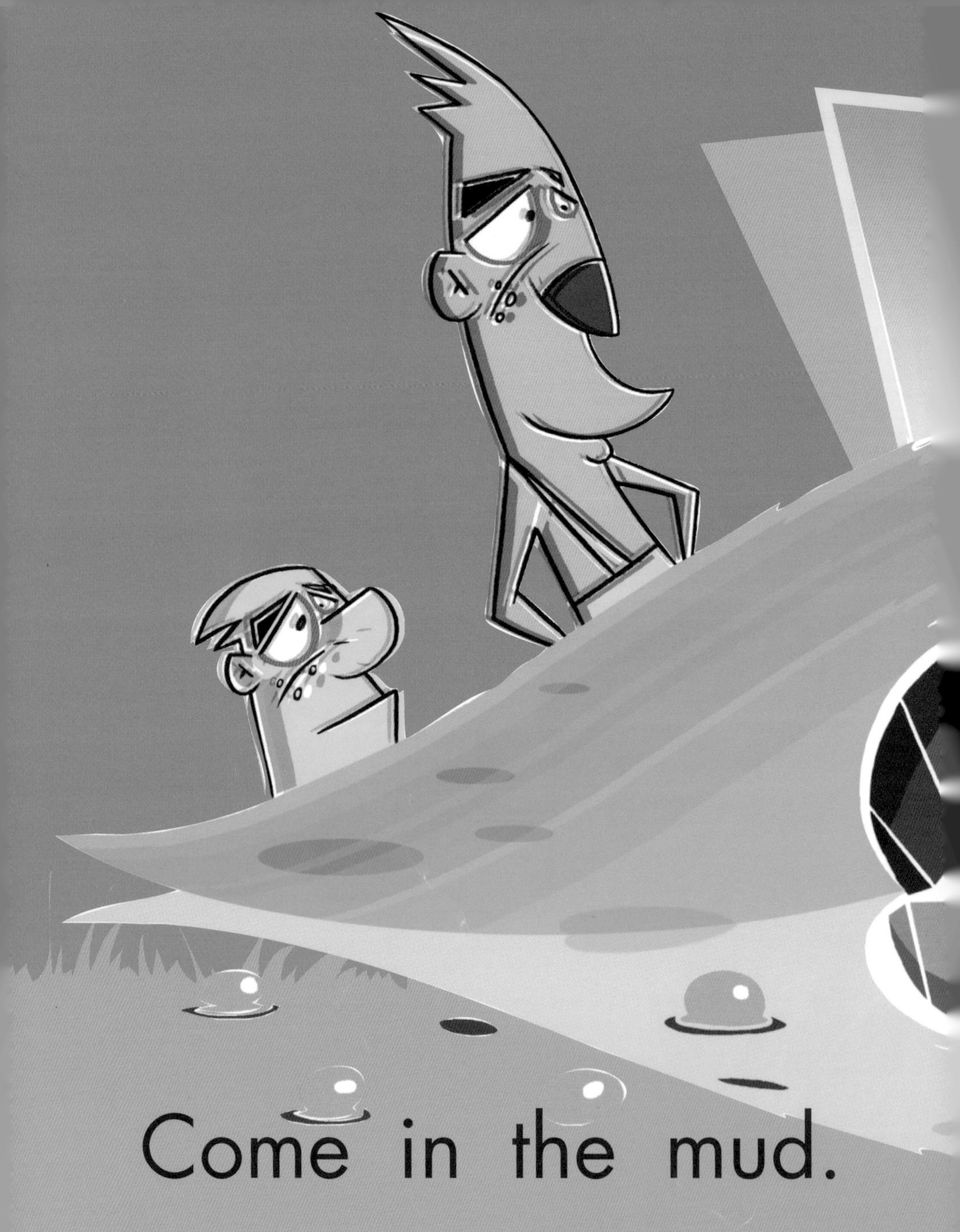

Come in the mud.

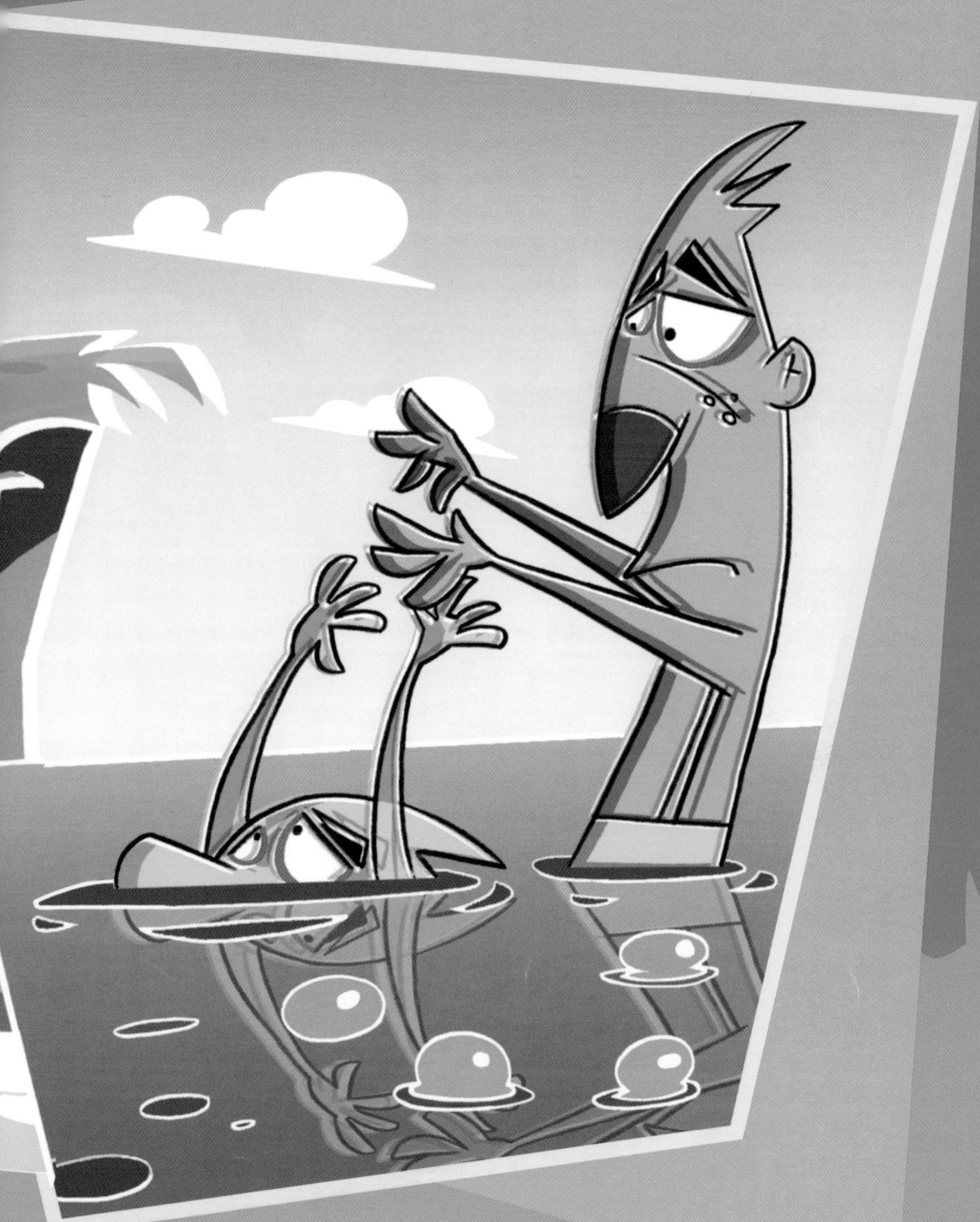

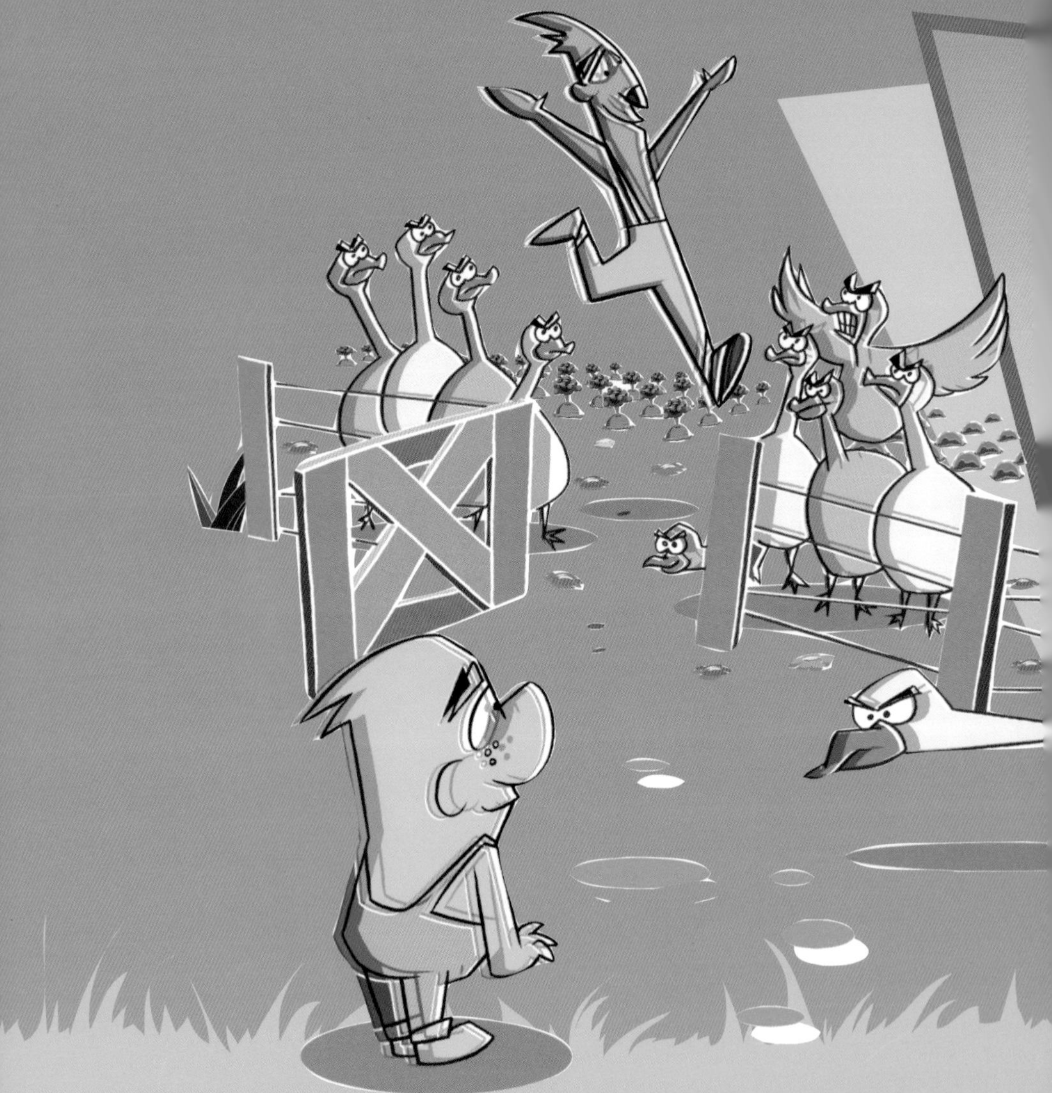

Come in the garden.

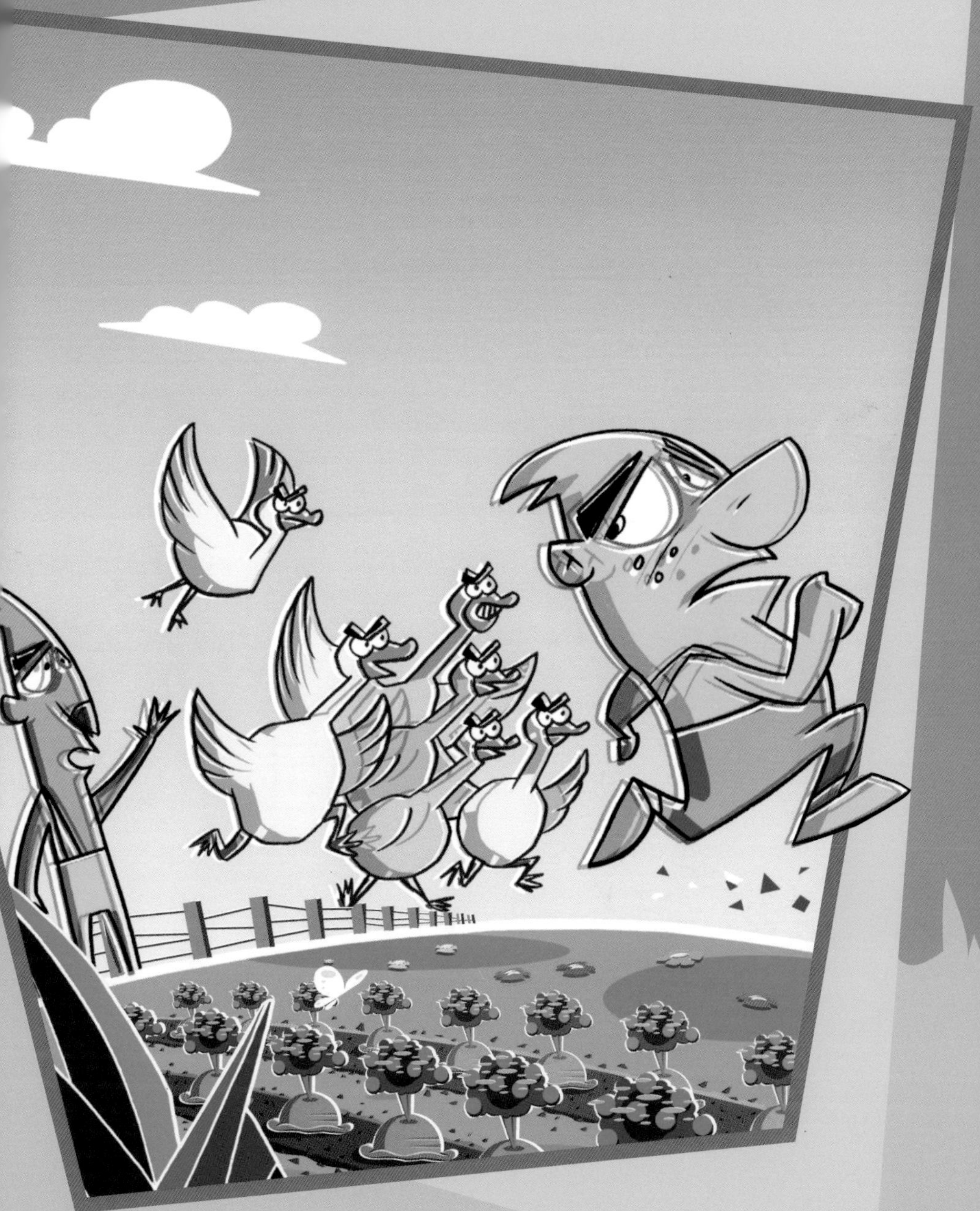

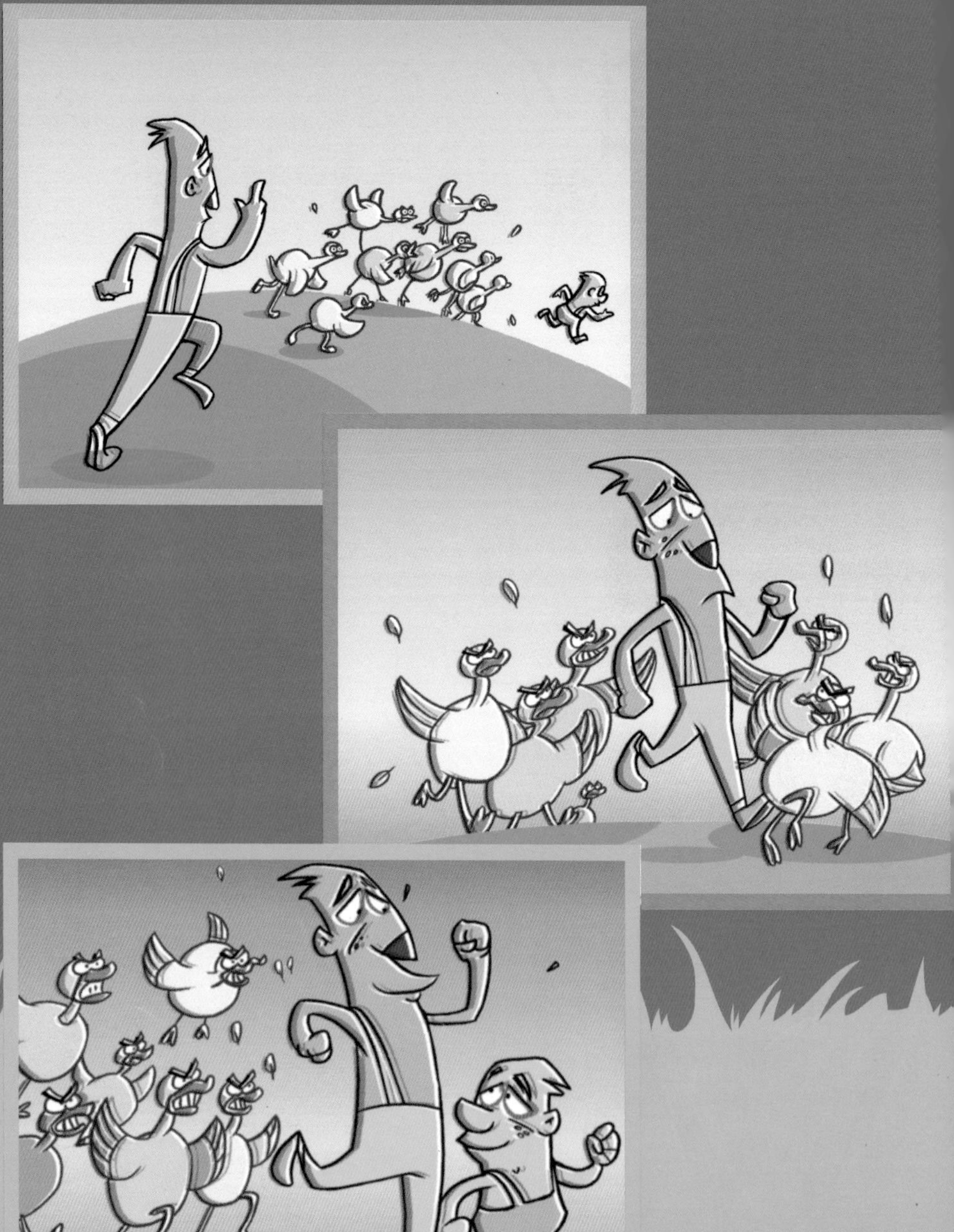

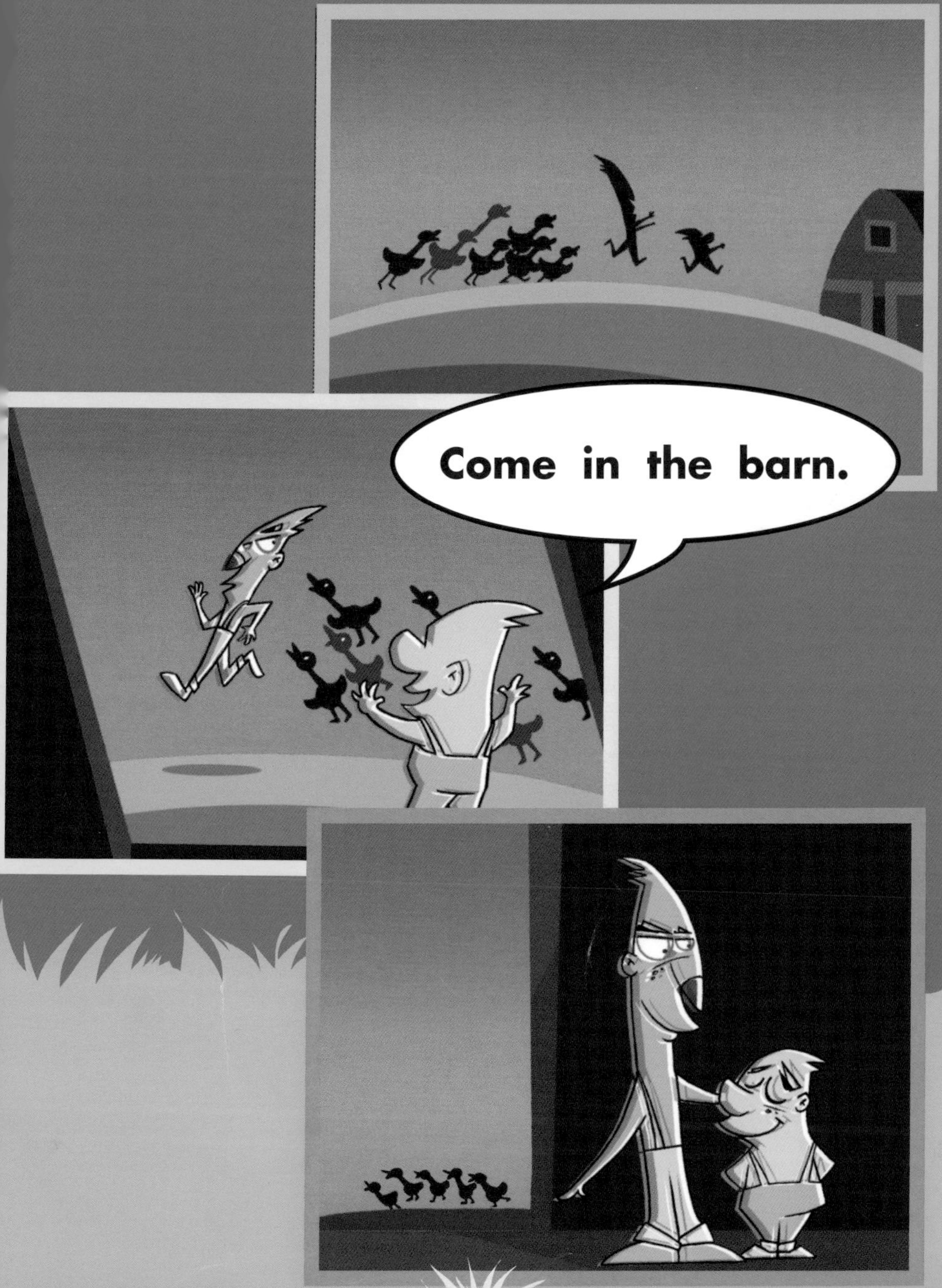
Come in the barn.

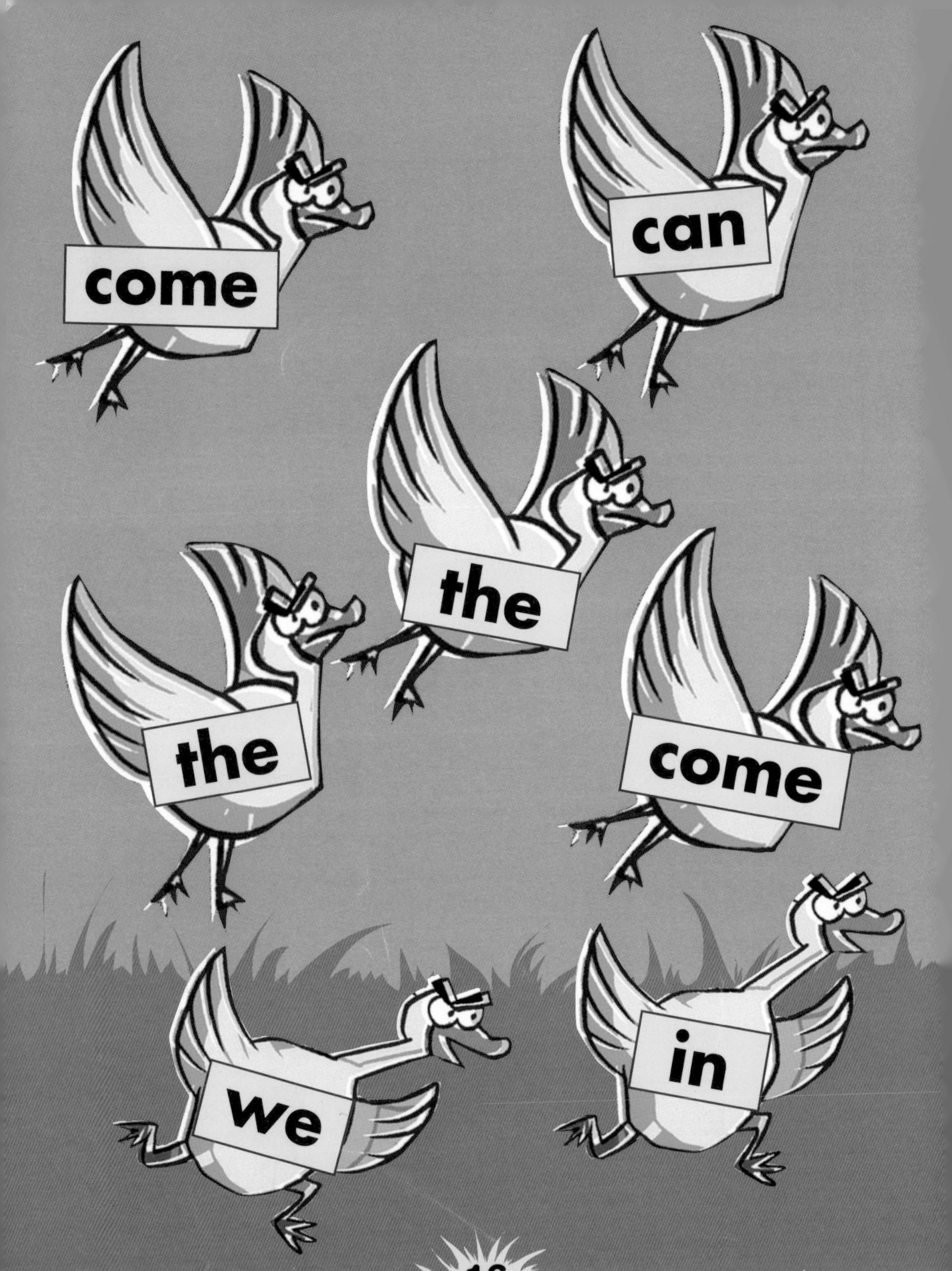
come
can
the
the
come
we
in